building
teamwork
in your marriage

homebuilders
COUPLES SERIES®

building
teamwork
in your marriage

by
robert lewis
&
david boehi

FAMILYLIFE®
Little Rock, Arkansas

BUILDING TEAMWORK IN YOUR MARRIAGE
FamilyLife Publishing®
5800 Ranch Drive
Little Rock, Arkansas 72223
1-800-FL-TODAY • FamilyLife.com

FLTI, d/b/a FamilyLife®, is a ministry of Campus Crusade for Christ International®

Scripture quotations are from The Holy Bible, English Standard Version, copyright © 2001 by Crossway Bibles, a division of Good News Publishers. Used by permission. All rights reserved.

ISBN: 978-1-60200-328-6

Design: Brand Navigation, LLC

Cover image: © iStockphoto.com/iofoto

Printed in the United States of America

15 14 13 12 11   4 5 6 7 8

Unless the Lord builds the house,
those who build it labor in vain.

Psalm 127:1

The HomeBuilders Couples Series®

Building Your Marriage to Last
Improving Communication in Your Marriage
Resolving Conflict in Your Marriage
Mastering Money in Your Marriage
Building Teamwork in Your Marriage
Growing Together in Christ
Building Up Your Spouse
Managing Pressure in Your Marriage

The HomeBuilders Parenting Series®

Improving Your Parenting
Establishing Effective Discipline for Your Children
Guiding Your Teenagers
Raising Children of Faith

welcome to homebuilders

Marriage should be enjoyed, not endured. It is meant to be a vibrant relationship between two people who love each other with passion, commitment, understanding, and grace. So secure is the bond God desires between a husband and a wife that he uses it to illustrate the magnitude of Christ's love for the church (Ephesians 5:25–33).

Do you have that kind of love in your marriage?

Relationships often fade over time as people drift apart—but only if the relationship is left unattended. We have a choice in the matter; our marriages don't have to grow dull. Perhaps we just need to give them some attention.

That's the purpose behind the HomeBuilders Couples Series— to provide you a way to give your marriage the attention it needs and deserves. This is a biblically based small-group study because, in the Bible, God has given the blueprint for building a loving and secure marriage. His plan is designed to enable a man and a woman to grow together in a mutually satisfying relationship and then to reach out to others with the love of Christ. Ignoring God's plan may lead to isolation and, in far too many cases, the breakup of the home.

Whether your marriage needs a complete makeover or just a few small adjustments, we encourage you to consult God's design. Although written nearly two thousand years ago, Scripture still speaks clearly and powerfully about the conflicts and challenges men and women face.

Do we really need to be part of a group? Couldn't we just go through this study as a couple?

While you could work through the study as a couple, you would miss the opportunity to connect with friends and to learn from one another's experiences. You will find that the questions in each session not only help you grow closer to your spouse, but they also create an environment of warmth and fellowship with other couples as you study together.

What does it take to lead a HomeBuilders group?

Leading a group is much easier than you may think, because the leader is simply a facilitator who guides the participants through the discussion questions. You are not teaching the material but are helping the couples discover and apply biblical truths. The special dynamic of a HomeBuilders group is that couples teach themselves.

The study guide you're holding has all the information and guidance you need to participate in or lead a HomeBuilders group. You'll find leader's notes in the back of the guide, and additional helps are posted online at FamilyLife.com/Resources.

What is the typical schedule?

Most studies in the HomeBuilders Couples Series are six to eight weeks long, indicated by the number of sessions in the guide. The sessions are designed to take sixty minutes in the group with a project for the couples to complete between sessions.

Isn't it risky to talk about your marriage in a group?

The group setting should be enjoyable and informative—and non-threatening. **THREE SIMPLE GROUND RULES** will help ensure that everyone feels comfortable and gets the most out of the experience:

1. Share nothing that will embarrass your spouse.
2. You may pass on any question you do not want to answer.
3. If possible, as a couple complete the HomeBuilders project between group sessions.

What other help does FamilyLife offer?

Our list of marriage and family resources continues to grow. Visit FamilyLife.com to learn more about our:

- Weekend to Remember® getaway, The Art of Marriage®, and other events;
- slate of radio broadcasts, including the nationally syndicated *FamilyLife Today®*, *Real FamilyLife with Dennis Rainey®*, and *FamilyLife This Week®*;
- multimedia resources for small groups, churches, and community networking;
- interactive products for parents, couples, small-group leaders, and one-to-one mentors; and
- assortment of blogs, forums, and other online connections.

Robert Lewis is executive producer of LifeReady®, high-impact video resources designed to prepare couples, parents, men, and women to embrace God's best for their marriages, families, and lives. He has authored numerous books and films, including the nationally recognized Men's Fraternity series: *Quest for Authentic Manhood, Winning at Work and Home,* and *The Great Adventure.* Robert serves on the board of trustees for Leadership Network. Married since 1971, Robert and his wife, Sherard, reside in Little Rock, Arkansas, and have four children and three grandchildren.

David Boehi is a senior editor at FamilyLife. He has written and edited numerous FamilyLife resources, including *Preparing for Marriage.* He also writes and edits articles for FamilyLife's Web site. He and his wife, Merry, live in Little Rock, Arkansas.

contents

on building teamwork in your marriage

To move forward as a true team, a couple must deal with improving their communication, resolving conflict, growing together spiritually, and much more. And while we recognize that all of this is more than one study can address, this course will raise some important and helpful questions:

- What is the foundation of teamwork?
- How can your differences be a strength?
- What role does servanthood play in marriage?
- What biblical responsibilities do husbands and wives have?
- How should you respond to each other's key responsibilities?
- How can the principle of teamwork be put into practice?

You're in for some stimulating conversations, and we pray that each of you will have the ability to approach this topic with a fresh and open mind as you examine what the Bible says about teamwork in marriage.

—Dennis & Barbara Rainey

1

The Basis of
Teamwork

God's Word provides the foundation upon which teamwork in marriage is built.

A Team Sport

Take turns introducing yourselves and answering one or two of the following questions:

- What is a team, group, or organization that you really admire? Why?
- What has been one of the best teams, clubs, groups, or organizations you have been a part of? Explain what made being a part of that team a good experience.
- If you were to compare marriage to a team sport, what sport would you choose and why?

blueprints

The Winning Edge

Although a married couple does not compete against other couples for a prize, in many ways a husband and wife constitute a team that battles against forces that tear at their marriage.

1. What elements are necessary to create a winning team in sports like baseball, basketball, soccer, or football?

2. What factors can cause a team, even a good team, not to reach its potential? Which of these factors also affect marriage?

3. What are some typical challenges that couples face in marriage that require teamwork?

Better Than One

God's Word has a lot to say about marriage and about how a husband and wife can work together as a team.

4. Read Ecclesiastes 4:9–12. How would you apply this passage to marriage?

5. What are some ways that "two are better than one" in marriage? In your relationship how have you seen your respective strengths and weaknesses work together to make you strong as a team?

homebuilders principle: God puts two people together in marriage who will complement each other and be stronger as a team than they would be as individuals.

Foundational Principles

To build a winning team in marriage, a husband and wife must hold fast to a few foundational principles. Without these, spouses will not operate well as a team and will grow isolated in their relationship.

The first principle is *shared goals.* A successful team must know what it wants to accomplish; the team must choose these goals wisely.

6. Pretend you are the coach of a youth-league soccer team. As you look at your players, you see a typical assortment: a couple of players are very good athletes, a couple of others look as if they may never kick a ball straight, and the rest are average.

   Men: What do you think would happen if the only goal you gave your team was to have fun? How might this goal affect your practices? Your players' attitudes? Your players' performance?

   Women: What do you think would happen if the only goal you gave your team was to win the league championship? How might this goal affect your practices? Your players' attitudes? Your players' performance?

7. What are some goals a couple might want for their marriage?

8. In the Sermon on the Mount, Jesus talks about what is important in the kingdom of God, and he challenges his followers to choose a path quite different from that followed by most people. Read Matthew 5:14–16; 6:25–26, 33. What does Jesus say about the goals we should set for our lives?

9. How do you think it would affect your marriage if you both sought to fulfill these goals with your whole heart?

homebuilders principle: The first foundation of a successful team in marriage is the shared purpose of serving God.

make a date

Set a time for you and your spouse to complete the HomeBuilders project together before the next group meeting. You will be asked at the next session to share an insight or experience from the project.

date _____ time _____

location _____

homebuilders project

On Your Own

Answer the following questions:

1. What are some challenges you are facing in your marriage that require you to work well as a team?

2. What are some things that keep your marriage team from reaching its potential?

3. Name one or two things that typically happen in your marriage when you don't work together as a team.

4. What are you now facing that you can't handle without help from your spouse?

5. What are some strengths your spouse brings to your marriage that you appreciate?

6. Look again at the passages about the purpose God calls us to in life (question 8 on page 7). What types of things can keep you from pursuing this purpose in your life?

With Your Spouse

1. Share your responses to the questions you answered on your own.

2. What is one task or challenge that you agree you can't accomplish alone? How can you work together to accomplish this?

3. Read Matthew 7:24–27. How does working together help build a solid foundation in your marriage?

4. Close your time in prayer. Ask God to help you as you seek to work together as a team.

Remember to take your calendar to the next session for Make a Date.

2

Equal, Yet
Different

While God has created men and women with unique differences, both have equal worth in Christ.

One Thing I've Learned . . .

Complete one of the following statements to tell about something you have learned from marriage. (Remember, don't share anything that would embarrass your spouse.)

- One thing marriage has taught me about the opposite sex is . . .
- One assumption I had going into marriage that I quickly discovered was mistaken was . . .
- One thing I've learned about relating to a spouse is that, whenever possible, you should . . .

After everyone has completed a sentence, discuss this question: How can these lessons be used to build teamwork in marriage?

Project Report

If you completed the HomeBuilders project from the first session, share one thing you learned.

blueprints

It's not hard to recognize that there are differences between men and women. But beyond the obvious physical differences, men and women are different from one another in a variety of other ways. However, *recognizing* these differences is one thing; *appreciating* these differences is quite another!

A Call to Understanding

In Genesis 1:27 we read, "So God created man in his own image, in the image of God he created him; male and female he created them." When God created the human race, he divided it into "male and female" and called them "very good" (verse 31).

1. From your observation what are some common, nonphysical ways that men and women are different?

2. Read 1 Peter 3:7. Why do you think husbands are called to be understanding, or considerate, with their wives? If this exhortation had been addressed to wives, how might it have been stated differently?

3. Practically, what are some ways a husband and wife can gain a better understanding of each other?

4. Why is it important for a husband and wife to understand the differences between men and women? When has such an understanding helped you in your marriage?

Different Functions, Equal Worth

5. Read 1 Corinthians 12:12–26. In what ways is marriage like a body—a unit that is made up of many parts?

6. Read 1 Peter 3:7 again. What do you think it means to regard your spouse as an heir "with you of the grace of life"?

7. What additional insight do you find in Galatians 3:25–29 about how all people are equal before God?

8. What do you think it means, practically, to be "one in Christ Jesus"? What effect should that have on how we relate to other Christians? On how we relate to our spouses?

9. What can happen in a marriage when one spouse does not regard the other as having equal worth before God?

homebuilders principle: True equality in a marriage is achieved when a husband and wife joyfully pursue unity in their diversity.

make a date

Set a time for you and your spouse to complete the HomeBuilders project together before the next group meeting. You will be asked at the next session to share an insight or experience from the project.

date _____ time _____

location _____

homebuilders project

On Your Own

Answer the following questions:

1. What insight, discovery, or reminder from this session did you find most helpful?

2. What is one difference between you and your spouse that you've grown to appreciate during your marriage?

3. What is one function your spouse provides that you often take for granted? What is one way you can honor him or her this week for that function?

4. List one or two things you would like your spouse to understand about you—things you feel he or she is unaware of
   because of your gender difference.

5. List an area in which you are having difficulty understanding
   your spouse.

6. In what ways do the things you just listed affect the quality
   of your marriage? How can you communicate these things
   in a kind and loving way?

7. What does it mean to you that you and your spouse can have
   different functions in marriage but still have equal worth in
   the eyes of God?

With Your Spouse

1. Start your time together by coming up with some examples
    of great combinations—two things (or people) that are better
    together than apart. For example, peanut butter and jelly
    make a great combination.

    After you have identified some great combinations, discuss
    these questions:

    - What are the characteristics of a great combination?

    - How do these characteristics apply—or not apply—to
      a marriage?

2. Read Colossians 3:12–17 together to set the tone for the rest
    of your discussion.

3. Share your responses to the questions you answered on your
    own.

4. Discuss some specific actions you can take as a couple to
    promote better understanding between you.

5. Pray together. Thank God for each other and for your
    differences.

Remember to take your calendar to the next session for Make a Date.

3

Following
Christ's Example

To rightly relate to each other, a husband and wife need to follow Christ's example of serving others.

warm-up

Who Does What?

During the next few minutes, write down a list of the household tasks for which you and your spouse regularly take responsibility. For example, if you typically mow the lawn and your spouse feeds the dog, list those tasks in the appropriate column on the following chart.

Husband	Wife

After compiling your lists, answer the following questions:

- What process, if any, did you go through as a couple to decide who would do what?

- What would happen in your marriage if you didn't have any set tasks or chores and instead negotiated each day about who would do what?

Project Report

Share one thing you learned from the HomeBuilders project from last session.

In the first two sessions, we looked at working together as a team and understanding, appreciating, and honoring each other's differences. In this session we will examine three more foundational teamwork principles. We find these principles illustrated by some surprising actions and words from Jesus.

Called to Love

1. According to the following passages, to what standards of love are we called?

   • Matthew 22:34–40

   • John 13:34–35

   • 1 Corinthians 13:1–3

   • 1 John 4:10–12

2. How is this love—the love of Christ—different from the love experienced in many marriages?

3. How do these passages challenge you regarding the love you have for your spouse?

🔲 **homebuilders principle:** A key element in building teamwork in marriage is loving your spouse as Christ loves you.

Called to Serve

4. Read John 13:1–17. What was Jesus trying to teach the disciples?

5. Why do you think Peter was so resistant to Jesus' actions?

6. Read Matthew 20:25–28 and Mark 9:33–35. In what way is Christ's description of a leader different from the way our world describes a leader?

7. What are some ways that Christ's example of servanthood can be practiced in marriage?

Called to Humility

8. Read Philippians 2:1–8, in which Paul expounds on the theme of humility. How do the actions described in this passage reflect the kind of humility Jesus modeled?

9. What happens in marriage when a spouse looks only to his or her self-interests?

10. How has your spouse recently displayed the attitude of Philippians 2—showing humility and not acting from selfishness, rivalry, or conceit?

homebuilders principle: In life and in marriage, Christ calls us to a radical concept—to serve others rather than ourselves.

make a date

Set a time for you and your spouse to complete the HomeBuilders project together before the next group meeting. You will be asked at the next session to share an insight or experience from the project.

date _____ time _____

location _____

homebuilders project

On Your Own

The importance of following Christ's example by loving and serving each other in marriage may become more apparent as you think about how your lives will change as you grow older. Using the following chart, think about the issues you will face individually and as a couple in the future. For example: What financial pressures do you think you will face? What will your daily schedule be like? What will be the likely state of your health? What career pressures or decisions will there be? If you have children or plan to have children, be sure to factor this in as well. Think of what ages your children will be and how the presence of children will affect you as a couple.

Record the issues you think you may face individually and as a couple in the years to come. Then, when you are together, you will compare charts and work on the last column.

	Issues we'll face individually	Issues we'll face as a couple	Ways we'll need to love and serve each other
Next 1-2 years			

	Issues we'll face individually	Issues we'll face as a couple	Ways we'll need to love and serve each other
5 years from now			
10 years from now			
More than 20 years from now			

With Your Spouse

1. Share your charts with each other.

2. Discuss and record ways you can love and serve each other.

3. Look back at the "Who Does What?" chart in the Warm-Up (page 20). As you consider your regular household tasks in light of Christ's call to love and serve each other, what adjustments could you make in your responsibilities?

4. Close in prayer, asking God for wisdom and help in serving each other.

Remember to take your calendar to the next session for Make a Date.

4

Biblical
Responsibilities

A couple that is serious about pleasing God will shape their marriage around the scriptural responsibilities for husbands and wives.

Meeting Needs

In our last session we talked about the importance of considering each other's needs as more important than our own (Philippians 2:1–8). Everyone has needs, but some needs are of greater importance to women than they are to men—and vice versa.

Women: Share what you believe are some special needs that women have in their marriages. Men, listen carefully and take notes!

Men: Share what you believe are some special needs that men have in their marriages. Women, listen carefully and take notes!

Now read Ephesians 5:33. What are husbands told to do? What are wives told to do? What are some practical ways you can demonstrate these respective attitudes toward each other?

Project Report

Share one thing you learned from the HomeBuilders project from last session.

An Overall Perspective

As we have learned in previous sessions, it is important to know a number of foundational principles about teamwork in marriage:

- Two can work better than one.
- God sets up many situations in which team members have different functions but equal worth.
- We all are called to love and serve one another.

With these principles in mind, we now turn to the different responsibilities for husbands and for wives, as described in the Bible. In time, every marriage settles into some social and organizational arrangement. Husband and wife assume specific responsibilities that uphold the arrangement.

It is important to note that there is often great misunderstanding concerning what the Bible says about the different functions and responsibilities a husband and wife should assume in a marriage. Therefore it is extremely important that you don't jump to conclusions about what this session and the next one will teach. The responsibilities for husbands and wives should not be viewed as comprehensive lifestyles. In other words, while these responsibilities are important, they do not cover all that one does. There is room for great latitude, creativity, and flexibility regarding one's responsibilities in marriage.

In Ephesians 5:21, Paul instructs us to submit to one another "out of reverence for Christ." This instruction echoes the passages we studied in the last session about our call to love, to humility, and to servanthood. But Paul doesn't stop there. In the remainder of the chapter, he describes how this submission looks for different people.

1. In two groups of roughly equal size, read Ephesians 5:22–33. Then answer the following questions:

   - As a husband or a wife, what strikes you about this passage?

   - To what extent do you believe the passage's instructions are relevant to husbands and wives today?

A Husband's Key Responsibilities

2. Reread Ephesians 5:22–27. What is your understanding of Paul's statement "for the husband is the head of the wife"?

3. What dangers or misunderstandings are possible with the concept of headship?

4. In the last session we looked at how Jesus led. Read Luke 22:25–27. What styles of leadership does Jesus contrast? Against which of these styles do people react? Why?

5. Look again at Ephesians 5:25–27, 31–32. What do you think it means for a husband to love his wife "as Christ loved the church and gave himself up for her"? What would this kind of love look like in a marriage relationship?

A Wife's Response

Many Christians believe a wife's role in marriage is to submit to her husband. However, submission may more appropriately be seen as a *response* rather than a role.

6. Read the following verses:

   - Ephesians 5:21–24
   - Colossians 3:18
   - 1 Peter 3:1–6

   What do you think it means to submit or to be submissive? What emotions does the concept of submission evoke in many people?

7. Why do you think Scripture mentions the church's submission to Christ as a model for a wife's submission to her husband?

8. If a husband is fulfilling his biblical responsibilities, what effect will this likely have on his wife's attitude about submission?

9. How do you think submission can be demonstrated in marriage? Under what circumstances should a wife not submit to her husband? Why?

10. Any discussion about biblical responsibilities in marriage can lead to sharp disagreements. People bring to the debate their own views shaped by experience, their childhoods, and prevailing cultural philosophies. From what we've learned so far about how God views teamwork in marriage, how would you respond to the following statements?

"Marriages should be like they were when I was growing up—you know, traditional. The man should bring home the bacon, and the woman should fry it up in the pan."

"Essentially, the institution of marriage exists to oppress women. I mean, a woman gets married and is supposed to change her name? It's like you're not your own person anymore. A woman is equal to a man and shouldn't lower herself to the subjection of marriage."

"Marriage should be an equal partnership. The only specific responsibilities a husband or wife should assume are ones that have been mutually agreed upon, based on each other's gifts and abilities."

 homebuilders principle: The husband is called to a servant-leadership responsibility in marriage.

make a date

Set a time for you and your spouse to complete the HomeBuilders project together before the next group meeting. You will be asked at the next session to share an insight or experience from the project.

date _____ time _____

location _____

homebuilders project

On Your Own

Answer the following questions:

1. As you look back over this session, what is one idea you can apply to be a better teammate in your marriage?

2. Read again Luke 22:25–27. Using the following chart, write down how you think a serving leader and a lording leader would handle these everyday situations. Be specific.

Lording Leader	Situation	Serving Leader
Example: Buys what pleases him. Is impulsive. Does not ask for or take into consideration his wife's insights. Overlooks her needs and the needs of his family.	Purchasing a major item	Example: Deliberates with his wife before making such a decision. Considers her feelings. Exalts the needs of his wife and family above his own.

Lording Leader	Situation	Serving Leader
	Fulfilling responsibilities around the home	
	Disciplining the children	
	Listening to his wife's suggestions	
	Handling finances	
	Making a difficult decision	
	Engaging in spiritual initiatives: prayer, church, Bible study, etc.	

3. Husbands, write down how you feel about the responsibilities set forth in this session. What one adjustment could you make right now that would help you fulfill God's purpose?

4. Wives, give an example of how you have seen your husband fulfill his biblical responsibilities.

With Your Spouse

1. Share your responses to the questions you answered on your own.

2. So far we have considered four foundational principles for building teamwork in marriage:

   - We are to pursue biblical goals together.
   - People can assume different functions yet still have equal worth.
   - We are to show Christlike love to each other.
   - Christ calls us to radical servanthood in our marriage relationship.

Based on what you have studied in this session, discuss how these biblical principles are important to remember when you look at the differing responsibilities of a husband and a wife.

3. Read Psalm 127:1. Discuss how this verse relates to the structure of your marriage.

4. Pray, asking God to help you understand and fulfill your God-given responsibilities as husband and wife.

Remember to take your calendar to the next session for Make a Date.

5

Biblical
Responses

A woman's responsibilities in marriage, though different from a man's, are equally important.

warm-up

Voices

As mentioned in the previous session, every marriage will settle into some social and organizational arrangement. What structure a couple decides upon is largely determined by the "voices" to which they listen. Review the list of voices below that are influential in structuring a marriage. Which of these have most influenced your life? Rank them 1–6, using 1 to represent the most influential and 6 as the least influential.

__ How I saw my parents live out their marriage
__ What I have absorbed from the culture

__ How my peers have structured their marriages

__ What I understand the Bible to teach about marriage

__ What I have studied, read in books, or learned in school

__ Other:

Up to this point in your life, what has been your vision of your key responsibilities in marriage? In what way, if any, has this changed during this study?

Project Report

Share one thing you learned from the HomeBuilders project from last session.

A Wife's Key Responsibilities

1. Read Genesis 2:18–22. What words or images come to mind when you think of a wife as a husband's "helper"?

2. Read how God is described in Psalm 10:14, Psalm 118:7, and Isaiah 41:10, 13–14. Considering these verses, how do you think God views the role of helper?

3. Read Proverbs 31:10–31 and Titus 2:3–5. What perspectives do these passages add to your understanding of a wife's responsibilities?

4. What do you think is meant by the words "working at home" in Titus 2:5, as related to a wife's responsibilities?

5. Proverbs 31 describes the wife as engaged both in business (verses 16 and 18) and in looking after her household (verses 15 and 27). Which of these undertakings do you believe is most reflective of a wife's responsibilities? Why?

A Husband's Response

Just as Scripture calls for a wife to respond to her husband's responsibilities, it also requires a husband to respond to his wife's responsibilities.

6. An often-neglected aspect of a husband's call to love his wife is how that love is demonstrated. Read the following scriptures:

   - Ephesians 5:28–29
   - Colossians 3:19
   - 1 Peter 3:7

   In these verses, what key words or admonishments describe the kind of response a wife needs from her husband?

7. Read Proverbs 31:28–31. Based on these verses, what should be the husband's response to his wife?

8. Why is a husband's praise important to a wife's success in fulfilling her biblical responsibilities?

9. What could happen in a marriage in which a wife does not receive encouragement or praise from her husband?

10. What are some practical ways these responsibilities can be demonstrated in marriage?

homebuilders principle: The wife is called to fulfill the responsibilities of helping her husband and of making her home a priority.

make a date

Set a time for you and your spouse to complete the HomeBuilders project together before the next group meeting. You will be asked at the next session to share an insight or experience from the project.

date _____ time _____

location _____

homebuilders project

On Your Own

Answer the following questions:

1. As you have studied and discussed responsibilities and responses in marriage during the past two sessions, what is one way you have been challenged?

2. Read the designated scenarios, and respond to the questions that follow.

For husbands:

#1: Chuck is an old-school, take-charge kind of guy. In his office hangs a poster with a saying that serves as his motto: Lead, follow, or get out of the way. Chuck is results oriented and is accustomed to getting things done his way. For the most part, his aggressive style of leadership has served him well in the business world. But at home, that's a different story. Chuck expects the same lockstep obedience from his wife and kids that he gets from his subordinates at work. This expectation has caused ongoing tension between him and his wife. When his wife disagrees with him, he often tells her, "The Good Book says I'm the head of this house."

#2: Ron has the exact opposite personality of his wife, Becky. While she is outgoing and talkative, he is quiet and reserved. For the most part, they complement each other well. However, Ron struggles with being a spiritual leader in his home. From his perspective, Becky prays better than he does and is more spiritual than he is. *What can I do to lead?* he asks himself.

- Of the examples of Chuck and Ron, whom can you relate to more? Why?

- In what ways do Chuck and Ron need to change?

- What is your biggest challenge in fulfilling your biblical responsibilities as a husband?

For wives:

#1: Karla is thirty-four and has been married four years. Her husband, Blair, is a successful stockbroker, and she is happy and fulfilled in her work as a marketing consultant. She and her husband are thinking of beginning a family, but she is hesitant because of the impact it would have on her career.

#2: Maria is a stay-at-home mom with three children. She is grateful to her husband for many things, including his love for his children and his ability to provide for them. She struggles, however, with his behavior when he returns home on work nights. Typically he settles into his easy chair and hardly budges except for dinner. He does little to help with the children or with household chores—he thinks that's her job. Maria is exhausted, and sometimes she feels like a single parent.

- How would you advise these women regarding their biblical responsibilities?

- What is your biggest challenge in fulfilling your biblical responsibilities as a wife?

3. To this point in your marriage, what grade would you give yourself for supporting your spouse in his or her responsibilities in marriage? Explain.

4. What is one change you could make to better support your spouse and improve your grade?

5. What is one practical way your spouse could help you fulfill your responsibilities as a husband or wife?

With Your Spouse

1. Share your responses to the questions you answered on your own.

2. Read Proverbs 31:10–31 and discuss the following:

- How would you characterize the relationship between the husband and wife in this passage?
- In what way is the relationship that passage describes like or unlike your relationship?
- Which traits would you like to see reflected more in your relationship? How can you accomplish this?

3. If you have come to recognize shortcomings in the way you have handled your responsibilities in your marriage or in the way you have responded to your spouse's responsibilities, apologize to each other in a humble and loving way.

4. Close in prayer together, asking God to help you as you seek to properly respond to and support each other.

Remember to take your calendar to the next session for Make a Date.

6

Making Teamwork
Work

Through the power of the Holy Spirit, spouses can apply the principles of teamwork in their marriage.

Checking In

Complete one or both of the following phrases:

- This course has helped our teamwork by . . .
- One thing I want to change about myself as a result of this study is . . .

Project Report

Share one thing you learned from the HomeBuilders project from the last session.

blueprints

Having discussed biblical responsibilities and responses for husbands and wives, let's see how these concepts might apply to everyday living.

Responsibilities, Responses, and the Real World

1. Michael and Jessica are expecting their first child. Both agree that it would be ideal if Jessica could quit her job and become a stay-at-home mother. However, they are concerned about whether they could make ends meet, as they depend on both incomes.

    • What do you think Michael and Jessica should do?

    • In what way do biblical responsibilities and responses play into this scenario?

2. James is not afraid to say what he thinks. Often this trait is an asset, but it also leads him into conflict on a regular basis. For example, his wife, Amanda, doesn't like going out to eat at a nice restaurant because she knows that he will probably antagonize the waiter by making critical comments and unrealistic demands.

This year their oldest son began playing on a Little League baseball team, and it didn't take long for James to stir up conflict in this new arena. He argues with coaches about their strategies and the amount of playing time his son gets.

If Amanda tries to talk to her husband about his behavior, he becomes angry. When she asks friends at church what she should do, some urge her to boldly confront him, while others counsel her by saying, "Just pray, because it's not right for you to tell him what he's doing wrong. He's the head of the home, and you're supposed to submit to him."

- What do you think Amanda should do?

- In what way do biblical responsibilities and responses play into this scenario?

3. Daniel and Stephanie have been married eight years and
   have two children, ages one and three. Daniel provides for
   the family's needs through his work as a corporate lawyer,
   and Stephanie is a full-time mother.

   Their problems begin when Daniel arrives home at night. He
   is tired from a busy day at work and wants to relax in his
   favorite chair in front of the television for a while. Stephanie,
   meanwhile, finds it difficult to prepare their dinner while
   also supervising the kids. Daniel plays with the children each
   night after dinner, but about the time they need to get ready
   for bed, he usually goes into his den and either makes work-
   related phone calls or completes some paperwork.

   Stephanie is tired of this routine, and he is tired of her com-
   plaining. "I'm doing my job, and you're doing yours," he says.

   - What do you think should happen in this relationship?

   - In what way do biblical responsibilities and responses
     play into this scenario?

4. Thinking back over your marriage, what is one situation you might handle differently now, based on your current understanding of biblical responsibilities in marriage?

5. When you reflect on what has been discussed in this course about building teamwork in marriage, what is the most difficult thing for you to apply?

Succeeding in the Spirit

It's easy to feel overwhelmed when you look at what God says about marriage. It may seem impossible for you to make it work. But, of course, that is true of the Christian life in general. And that's why God offers help.

6. Read John 14:15–26. What promise does Jesus make to his followers? What insights do these verses give about the Holy Spirit?

7. Within all of us is a natural inclination to go our own way, to reject God's direction and resist God's help. This streak of independence, which found its way into the heart of humanity when Adam and Eve first disobeyed God, has been passed along to all subsequent generations.

   What do the following verses say about our natural inclination, our sinful nature?

   - Romans 7:18–21

   - Romans 8:5–8

   - Galatians 5:19–21a

8. Of the various ways the sinful nature influences us, which do you feel is most harmful to teamwork in marriage? Why?

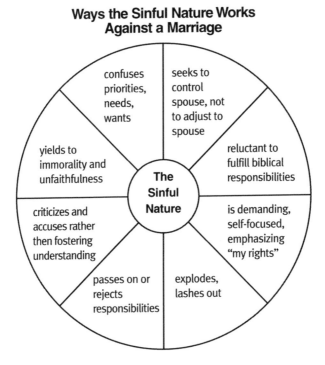

Ways the Sinful Nature Works Against a Marriage

confuses priorities, needs, wants

seeks to control spouse, not to adjust to spouse

yields to immorality and unfaithfulness

The Sinful Nature

reluctant to fulfill biblical responsibilities

criticizes and accuses rather then fostering understanding

is demanding, self-focused, emphasizing "my rights"

passes on or rejects responsibilities

explodes, lashes out

Defeating Selfishness

God has placed the Holy Spirit within every Christian so that our sinful natures can be opposed and overcome. Having two opposing forces vying for our obedience creates an ongoing internal conflict, which most of us feel every day.

9. Read the following passages:

   - Romans 6:12–14
   - Romans 8:5–8

- Romans 12:1–2
- Galatians 5:16–18

What do these verses say about our choices in this battle?

Ways the Holy Spirit Works in a Marriage

The Holy Spirit

promotes the priority of raising God-honoring children

seeks the best for both husband and wife

clarifies priorities and needs from impulsive wants

guides according to the will of God

encourages forgiveness and understanding between a couple

helps one to fulfill biblical responsibilities

convicts of selfishness, thoughts or acts of impurity, immorality, and outbursts of anger

recalls what God's Word says in crucial moments of a marriage

10. Refer to the diagram showing the benefits of the Holy Spirit in marriage. Which of these benefits could you use the most right now in your life or marriage?

homebuilders principle: The Holy Spirit can equip you to fulfill what God desires for you in marriage.

make a date

Set a time for you and your spouse to complete the last HomeBuilders project of the study.

date _____ time _____

location _____

homebuilders project

On Your Own

Answer the following questions:

1. During the first meeting of this study, what expectations did you have for this course? How did your experience compare to your expectations?

2. What has been the best part of this study for you?

3. How have the principles you've studied in this course helped you build teamwork in your marriage?

4. As you look back, what action do you need to follow up on?

5. In what aspect of your life or marriage do you most need to experience the power of the Holy Spirit right now?

6. What might be hindering the Holy Spirit's work in your life?

7. Pray, and confess to God any sin that is hindering the Holy Spirit's work in your life. Ask God to help you walk in the Spirit.

With Your Spouse

1. Share your responses to the questions you answered on your own.

2. Evaluate some things you might do to continue building teamwork in your marriage, building up each other, and building up other people. For example, consider regularly setting aside time together, as you have for these Home-Builders projects. You may also want to consider some ideas from page 63 in "Where Do You Go from Here?"

3. Pray, asking the Lord for help through the Holy Spirit as you seek to continue building teamwork in your marriage.

where do you go from here?

We hope that you have benefited from this study in the Home-Builders Couples Series and that your marriage will continue to grow as you both submit your lives to Jesus Christ and build according to his blueprints. We also hope that you will reach out to strengthen other marriages in your local church and community. Your influence is needed.

A favorite World War II story illustrates this point clearly.

The year was 1940. The French army had just collapsed under Hitler's onslaught. The Dutch had folded, overwhelmed by the Nazi regime. The Belgians had surrendered. And the British army was trapped on the coast of France in the channel port of Dunkirk.

Two hundred twenty thousand of Britain's finest young men seemed doomed to die, turning the English Channel red with their blood. The Fuehrer's troops, only miles away in the hills of France, didn't realize how close to victory they actually were.

Any attempt at rescue seemed futile in the time remaining. A thin British navy—the professionals—told King George VI that they could save 17,000 troops at best. The House of Commons was warned to prepare for "hard and heavy tidings."

Politicians were paralyzed. The king was powerless. And the Allies could only watch as spectators from a distance. Then as the doom of the British army seemed imminent, a strange fleet appeared on the horizon of the English Channel—the wildest assortment of boats perhaps ever assembled in history. Trawlers, tugs, scows, fishing sloops, lifeboats, pleasure craft, smacks and coasters, sailboats, even the London fire-brigade flotilla. Ships manned by civilian volunteers—English fathers joining in the rescue of Britain's exhausted, bleeding sons.

William Manchester writes in his epic novel *The Last Lion* that what happened in 1940 at Dunkirk seems like a miracle. Not only were most of the British soldiers rescued but 118,000 other Allied troops as well.

Today the Christian home is much like those troops at Dunkirk— pressured, trapped, demoralized, and in need of help. The Christian community may be much like England—waiting for professionals to step in and save the family. But the problem is much too large for them to solve alone.

We need an all-out effort by men and women "sailing" to rescue the exhausted and wounded families. We need an outreach effort by common couples with faith in an uncommon God. For too long, married couples within the church have abdicated to those in full-time vocational ministry the privilege and responsibility of influencing others.

We challenge you to invest your lives in others, to join in the rescue. You and other couples around the world can team together to build thousands of marriages and families and, in doing so, continue to strengthen your own.

Be a HomeBuilder

Here are some practical ways you can make a difference in families today:

- Gather a group of four to seven couples and lead them through this HomeBuilders study. Consider challenging others in your church or community to form additional HomeBuilders groups.
- Commit to continue building marriages by doing another small-group study in the HomeBuilders Couples Series.
- Consider using the *JESUS* film as an outreach. For more information contact FamilyLife at the number or Web site below.
- Host a dinner party. Invite families from your neighborhood to your home, and as a couple share your faith in Christ.
- If you have attended FamilyLife's Weekend to Remember marriage getaway, consider offering to assist your pastor in counseling engaged couples, using the material you received.

For more information about these ministry opportunities, contact your local church or

FamilyLife
PO Box 7111
Little Rock, AR 72223
1-800-FL-TODAY
FamilyLife.com

our problems, God's answers

Every couple has to deal with problems in marriage—communication problems, money problems, difficulties with sexual intimacy, and more. Learning how to handle these issues is important to cultivating a strong and loving relationship.

The Big Problem

One basic problem is at the heart of every other problem in marriage, and it's too big for any person to deal with on his or her own. The problem is separation from God. If you want to experience life and marriage the way they were designed to be, you need a vital relationship with the God who created you.

But sin separates us from God. Some try to deal with sin by working hard to become better people. They may read books on how to control anger, or they may resolve to stop cheating on their taxes, but in their hearts they know—we all know—that the sin problem runs much deeper than bad habits and will take more than our best behavior to overcome it. In reality, we have rebelled against God. We have ignored him and have decided to run our lives in a way that makes sense to us, thinking that our ideas and plans are better than his.

> For all have sinned and fall short of the glory of God.
> (Romans 3:23)

What does it mean to "fall short of the glory of God"? It means that none of us has trusted and treasured God the way we should. We have sought to satisfy ourselves with other things and have treated them as more valuable than God. We have gone our own way. According to the Bible, we have to pay a penalty for our sin. We cannot simply do things the way we choose and hope it will be okay with God. Following our own plans leads to our destruction.

> There is a way that seems right to a man, but its end
> is the way to death. (Proverbs 14:12)

> For the wages of sin is death. (Romans 6:23)

The penalty for sin is that we are separated from God's love. God is holy, and we are sinful. No matter how hard we try, we cannot come up with some plan, like living a good life or even trying to do what the Bible says, and hope that we can avoid the penalty.

God's Solution to Sin

Thankfully, God has a way to solve our dilemma. He became a man through the person of Jesus Christ. Jesus lived a holy life in perfect obedience to God's plan. He also willingly died on a cross to pay our penalty for sin. Then he proved that he is more powerful than sin or death by rising from the dead. He alone has the power to over-rule the penalty for our sin.

> Jesus said to him, "I am the way, and the truth, and the
> life. No one comes to the Father except through me."
> (John 14:6)

But God shows his love for us in that while we were still sinners, Christ died for us. (Romans 5:8)

For the wages of sin is death, but the free gift of God is eternal life in Christ Jesus our Lord. (Romans 6:23)

The death and resurrection of Jesus have fixed our sin problem. He has bridged the gap between God and us. He is calling us to come to him and to give up our flawed plans for running our lives. He wants us to trust God and his plan.

Accepting God's Solution

If you recognize that you are separated from God, he is calling you to confess your sins. All of us have made messes of our lives because we have stubbornly preferred our ideas and plans to his. As a result, we deserve to be cut off from God's love and his care for us. But God has promised that if we will acknowledge that we have rebelled against his plan, he will forgive us and will fix our sin problem.

But to all who did receive him, who believed in his name, he gave the right to become children of God. (John 1:12)

For by grace you have been saved through faith. And this is not your own doing; it is the gift of God, not a result of works, so that no one may boast. (Ephesians 2:8–9)

When the Bible talks about receiving Christ, it means we acknowledge that we are sinners and that we can't fix the problem ourselves. It means we turn away from our sin. And it means we trust Christ to forgive our sins and to make us the kind of people he wants us to be. It's not enough to intellectually believe that Christ is the Son of God. We must trust in him and his plan for our lives by faith, as an act of the will.

Are things right between you and God, with him and his plan at the center of your life? Or is life spinning out of control as you seek to make your own way?

If you have been trying to make your own way, you can decide today to change. You can turn to Christ and allow him to transform your life. All you need to do is talk to him and tell him what is stirring in your mind and in your heart. If you've never done this, consider taking the steps listed here:

- Do you agree that you need God? Tell God.
- Have you made a mess of your life by following your own plan? Tell God.
- Do you want God to forgive you? Tell God.
- Do you believe that Jesus' death on the cross and his resurrection from the dead gave him the power to fix your sin problem and to grant you the free gift of eternal life? Tell God.
- Are you ready to acknowledge that God's plan for your life is better than any plan you could come up with? Tell God.
- Do you agree that God has the right to be the Lord and Master of your life? Tell God.

Seek the LORD while he may be found; call upon him while he is near. (Isaiah 55:6)

Here is a suggested prayer:

Lord Jesus, I need you. Thank you for dying on the cross for my sins. I receive you as my Savior and Lord. Thank you for forgiving my sins and giving me eternal life. Make me the kind of person you want me to be.

The Christian Life

For the person who is a follower of Christ—a Christian—the penalty for sin is paid in full. But the effect of sin continues throughout our lives.

> If we say we have no sin, we deceive ourselves, and the truth is not in us. (1 John 1:8)

> For I do not do the good I want, but the evil I do not want is what I keep on doing. (Romans 7:19)

The effects of sin carry over into our marriages as well. Even Christians struggle to maintain solid, God-honoring marriages. Most couples eventually realize they can't do it on their own. But with God's help, they can succeed.

To learn more, read the extended version of this article at FamilyLife.com/Resources.

leader's notes

What is the leader's job?

Your role is more of a facilitator than a teacher. A teacher usually does most of the talking and instructing whereas a facilitator encourages people to think and to discover what Scripture says. You should help group members feel comfortable and keep things moving forward.

Is there a structure to the sessions?

Yes, each session is composed of the following categories:

Warm-Up (5–10 minutes): The purpose of Warm-Up is to help people unwind from a busy day and get to know one another better. Typically the Warm-Up starts with an exercise that is fun but also introduces the topic of the session.

Blueprints (45–50 minutes): This is the heart of the study when people answer questions related to the topic of study and look to God's Word for understanding. Some of the questions are to be discussed between spouses and others with the whole group.

HomeBuilders Project (60 minutes): This project is the unique application that couples will work on between the group meetings. Each HomeBuilders project contains two sections: (1) On your own—questions for husbands and wives to answer individually and (2) With your spouse—an opportunity for couples to share their answers with each other and to make application in their lives.

In addition to these regular features, occasional activities are labeled "Picture This." These activities provide a more active or visual way to make a particular point.

What is the best setting and time schedule for this study?

This study is designed as a small-group, home Bible study. However, it can be adapted for more structured settings like a Sunday school class. Here are some suggestions for using this study in various settings:

In a small group

To create a friendly and comfortable atmosphere, we recommend you do this study in a home setting. In many cases the couple that leads the study also serves as host, but sometimes involving another couple as host is a good idea. Choose the option you believe will work best for your group, taking into account factors such as the number of couples participating and the location.

Each session is designed as a sixty-minute study, but we recommend a ninety-minute block of time to allow for more relaxed conversation and refreshments. Be sure to keep in mind one of the cardinal rules of a small group: good groups start *and* end on time. People's time is valuable, and your group will appreciate your respecting this.

In a Sunday school class

If you want to use the study in a class setting, you need to adapt it in two important ways: (1) You should focus on the content of the Blueprints section of each session. That is the heart of the session.

(2) Many Sunday school classes use a teacher format instead of a small-group format. If this study is used in a class setting, the class should adapt to a small-group dynamic. This will involve an inter-active, discussion-based format and may also require a class to break into multiple smaller groups.

What is the best size group?

We recommend from four to seven couples (including you and your spouse). If more people are interested than you can accommodate, consider asking someone to lead a second group. If you have a large group, you may find it beneficial to break into smaller subgroups on occasion. This helps you cover the material in a timely fashion and allows for optimum interaction and participation within the group.

What about refreshments?

Many groups choose to serve refreshments, which helps create an environment of fellowship. If you plan to include refreshments, here are a couple of suggestions: (1) For the first session (or two) you should provide the refreshments. Then involve the group by having people sign up to bring them on later dates. (2) Consider starting your group with a short time of informal fellowship and refresh-ments (15–20 minutes). Then move into the study. If couples are late, they miss only the food and don't disrupt the study. You may also want to have refreshments available again at the end of your meeting to encourage fellowship. But remember to respect the group members' time by ending the session on schedule and allowing any-one who needs to leave to do so gracefully.

What about child care?

Groups handle this differently, depending on their needs. Here are a couple of options you may want to consider:

- Have people be responsible for making their own arrangements.
- As a group, hire someone to provide child care, and have all the children watched in one location.

What about prayer?

An important part of a small group is prayer. However, as the leader, you need to be sensitive to people's comfort level with praying in front of others. Never call on people to pray aloud unless you know they are comfortable doing this. You can take creative approaches, such as modeling prayer, calling for volunteers, and letting people state their prayers in the form of finishing a sentence. A helpful tool in a group is a prayer list. You should lead the prayer time, but allow another couple to create, update, and distribute prayer lists as their ministry to the group.

Find additional help and suggestions for leading your HomeBuilders group at FamilyLife.com/Resources.

about the leader's notes

The sessions in this study can be easily led without a lot of preparation time. However, accompanying Leader's Notes have been provided to assist you when needed. The categories within the Leader's Notes are as follows:

Objectives

The Objectives focus on the issues that will be presented in each session.

Notes and Tips

This section provides general ideas, helps, and suggestions about the session. You may want to create a checklist of things to include in each session.

Blueprints Commentary

This section contains notes that relate to the Blueprints questions. Not all Blueprints questions will have accompanying commentary notes. The number of the commentary note corresponds to the number of the question it relates to. (For example, the Leader's Notes, session 1, number 5 in the Blueprints Commentary section relates back to session 1, Blueprints, question 5.)

session one

the basis of teamwork

Objectives

God's Word provides the foundation upon which teamwork in marriage is built.

In this session couples will

- consider various elements that make for a good team,
- discuss goals for their marriage,
- identify love as the basis of teamwork in marriage.

Notes and Tips

1. If you have not already done so, you will want to read the information "About Leading a HomeBuilders Group" and "About the Leader's Notes," starting on page 75.

2. To further equip yourself for leading this course, you may want to get the book *Rocking the Roles: Building a Win-Win Marriage* by Robert Lewis and William D. Hendricks (Nav-Press, 1991). This book provides additional information on the topics discussed in this study.

3. As part of the first session, you may want to review with the group some ground rules (see page ix in "Welcome to HomeBuilders").

4. At this first meeting collect the names, phone numbers, and e-mail addresses of the group members. You may want to make a list that you can copy and distribute to the entire group.

5. Because this is the first session, make a special point to tell the group about the importance of the HomeBuilders project. Encourage each couple to make a date for a time before the next meeting to complete the project. Mention that you will ask about this during Warm-Up at the next session.

6. You may want to offer a closing prayer instead of asking others to pray aloud. Many people are uncomfortable praying in front of others, and unless you already know your group well, it may be wise to venture slowly into various methods of prayer. Regardless of how you decide to close, you should serve as a model.

7. If there is room for more, you may want to remind the group that because this study is just underway, they can still invite another couple to join the group.

Blueprints Commentary

Here is some additional information about various Blueprints questions. (Note: The numbers below correspond to the Blueprints questions they relate to.) If you share any of these points, be sure to do so in a manner that does not stifle discussion by making you the authority with the real answers. Begin your comments by saying things like, "One thing I notice in this passage is . . ." or, "I think another reason for this is . . ."

1. Suggest these responses if the group doesn't come up with something similar: good coaching, knowledge of the sport, and a proper understanding of what is required of each player.

2. One of the biggest factors that cause a husband and wife not to work together as a team is selfishness—our desire to go our own way and to be concerned primarily with meeting our own needs.

3. In responding to this question, challenge couples to think about the issues they have faced in their marriage that have required teamwork. If helpful to the discussion, you may want to mention that typical challenges can include deciding how to divide household tasks, such as cooking, cleaning, and managing finances; figuring how to work well together as parents; and caring for each other in times of sickness and tragedy.

6. If the only goal is to have fun, you may not accomplish much. The players may not learn very much about how to play the game, they may not learn much about teamwork, and you may have a difficult time enforcing discipline.

    To win the championship is a challenging goal, but you may be setting up your players for disappointment if this is the only goal, especially with this set of players. Too many factors must fall into place for a team to win a league championship, and many of those factors are out of your control. This may lead to frustration if things don't go well. You may be tempted to be overly harsh with your players, and they may feel too much pressure and might not enjoy the season at all.

Some examples of wise and realistic goals could be to teach your team the basic skills of the game, to teach them to play as a team, to make sure every player has a chance to contribute, to strive to play their best in each game, and to have fun while doing so.

8. These passages tell us that the goal of any Christian is to serve and glorify our Father in heaven. We should live in a way that allows God's light to show through us, and we should trust God to provide for our needs.

9. You may want to make the point that if a couple adopted these goals, they would have a common purpose in their marriage—working together to glorify God—and their whole perspective on life and marriage would change.

session two

equal, yet different

Objectives

While God has created men and women with unique differences, both have equal worth in Christ.

In this session couples will

- identify and discuss basic differences between men and women,
- examine their value and standing before God,
- work to better understand, appreciate, and honor each other's differences.

Notes and Tips

1. One of the subjects this session covers is the difference between men and women. This topic can be controversial because during the past few decades we've seen an ongoing debate about why men and women are different. Some have maintained that all differences other than obvious physical differences can be explained by how we are raised. However, mainstream scientific research now seems to agree that, while some differences between men and women are shaped by environment, other differences are part of our very nature.

Encourage a lively discussion on this topic, but keep comments focused on the fact that there are differences rather than on the source of those differences. In a marriage it's important to acknowledge, understand, and appreciate differences between a husband and wife, whether those differences are the result of gender or of interests and skills.

2. You may wish to have extra study guides and Bibles available for those who come to the session without them.

3. If someone joins the group for the first time in this session, give a brief summary of the main points of session 1. Also be sure to introduce people who do not know each other. You may want to have each new couple answer the Warm-Up question from session 1.

4. If refreshments are planned for this session, make sure arrangements for them have been made.

5. If your group has decided to use a prayer list, make sure this is covered.

6. You may want to ask for a volunteer or two to close the session in prayer. Check ahead of time with a couple of people you think might be comfortable praying aloud.

Blueprints Commentary

1. For this question, see point 1 of the preceding "Notes and Tips."

2. While husbands and wives have historically failed to understand and appreciate their differences, a case could be argued
   that husbands generally need to be exhorted more strongly
   in this area.

3. Understanding can come through honest study and discussion. Spouses should talk about their different needs, ways
   of relating to others, interests, and priorities.

4. Understanding their differences helps a husband and wife
   live and work together. Such understanding can also help a
   couple recognize and balance each other's strengths and
   weaknesses. If you don't understand the differences between
   you and your spouse, you will tend to assume that your
   spouse thinks, feels, and has the same needs you do.

5. While the most immediate application of 1 Corinthians
   12:12–26 is to the church, it is also easy to believe that in
   marriage some functions and gifts are superior to others.
   Yet this passage presents the crucial principle that, even
   though each of us has a different gift or function, all of us
   are equally important in the kingdom of God. No matter
   what function we have in marriage, we have equal worth
   before God.

7. Our faith gives us equal standing and equal worth before
   God. We are heirs of the same promises. If a husband and
   wife have received Christ as Savior, they have received the
   same salvation and the same blessings, and they can enjoy
   the same type of relationship with God. Some people believe

that Galatians 3:28 eliminates gender-role distinctions in marriage. However, it seems more likely that Paul is talking about our salvation in Christ.

8. We all have equal standing before God. In Christ he offers the same forgiveness, the same cleansing of sin to all.

9. If this issue isn't raised in the discussion, mention that this view will affect how one spouse treats the other. Such a view will also affect how a spouse regards each partner's responsibilities to create a working team in the marriage.

session three

following Christ's example

Objectives

To rightly relate to each other, a husband and wife need to follow Christ's example of serving others.

In this session couples will

- study the example Christ set for serving others,
- learn more about each other's needs,
- commit to a specific way to serve each other.

Notes and Tips

1. Congratulations! With the completion of this session, you will be halfway through this study. It's time for a checkup: How are you feeling? How is the group going? What has worked well so far? What things might you consider changing as you approach the remaining sessions?

2. Remember the importance of starting and ending on time.

3. You may want to make some notes right after the meeting to help evaluate how things went. Ask yourself questions such as, Did everyone participate? Is there anyone I should make a special effort to follow up with before the next session? Asking yourself questions like these will help you focus.

4. As a model to the group, you should complete the Home-Builders project.

Blueprints Commentary

4. Jesus was teaching about the importance of being a servant. Washing feet was a task relegated to servants.

5. Peter regarded Jesus as his master, so he was shocked that Jesus actually wanted to wash his feet. In Peter's mind, being a leader meant that others washed your feet, not vice versa.

6. Christ's idea of leadership is radically different. The world bestows power, privilege, praise, wealth, and status on its leaders. And those leaders often take advantage of others to bolster their standing. However, Jesus says that leaders should be servants. Some people may have difficulty reconciling serving with leading. You may need to state several times that almost everything in our society conditions us to view these terms as opposites. Jesus was truly revolutionary when he linked them together.

9. When you look only to your own interests in your relationship, you will grow isolated from each other.

session four

biblical responsibilities

Objectives

A couple that is serious about pleasing God will shape their marriage around the scriptural responsibilities for husbands and wives.

In this session couples will

- recognize that God has given certain unique responsibilities to husbands and wives,
- examine scriptural instructions about the key responsibilities of husbands and wives,
- define what they see as their key biblical responsibility.

Notes and Tips

1. This session tackles an issue that can be controversial—responsibilities of husbands and wives. Couples may not have a clear understanding of what the Bible says on this subject and may have preconceived ideas. Over the past few decades in our culture, the biblical models of responsibilities in marriage have been attacked, stereotyped, and ridiculed.

   Some people will have no problem accepting what the Bible says about these responsibilities, but others may.

Your goal is to encourage the group members to set aside preconceived notions and take an honest look at what these scriptures mean and how to apply them in marriage.

While this session examines passages related to responsibilities of husbands and wives, it does not attempt to deal with every responsibility in marriage addressed in the Bible. Rather, this session provides a general overview of what the Bible says and avoids specific issues such as physical intimacy and rearing children. The goal is to lay a foundation of understanding, challenging husbands and wives to consider their overall responsibilities in marriage.

2. Because of the subject matter, it is possible for a group to spend a lot of time discussing one question. Be wary of stifling good dialogue; however, it is important for you to politely keep things moving forward.

3. You and your spouse may want to write notes of thanks and encouragement to the couples in your group this week. Thank them for their commitment and contribution, and let them know you are praying for them. (Make a point to pray for them as you write their note.)

Blueprints Commentary

1. For the subgroups used with this question, consider breaking into groups of husbands and wives.

2. The exact definition of "head" as used in Ephesians 5:23 is debated by scholars. "Whether Paul intends the term to mean an authoritative ruler, or the first in a series, leader, servant-leader, or some other sense of 'head' is left open to debate. Of course, one important way of determining a metaphor's meaning is to check the surrounding context. Context along with other biblical references strongly suggest the servant-leader interpretation, in the authors' opinion" (*Rocking the Roles: Building a Win-Win Marriage*, Robert Lewis and William D. Hendricks, NavPress, 1991), 252.

Historically, it should be noted that Paul's statement in Ephesians 5:23 is not drawn from a culture where men reigned unchallenged as heads of their wives. In fact, a serious breakdown of marriage and family was occurring throughout the Roman Empire at this time.

3. Throughout history, many husbands have misunderstood the concept of headship and have used it for selfish ends. They have used it as an instrument of power and control and have subjugated their wives to various degrees. They have used the concept as the foundation for believing that men are superior to women. At the extreme, some have abused their wives emotionally and physically. This is not what the Bible teaches.

Some people cite the failure of husbands to properly exercise biblical headship as a reason to reject the entire idea of unique responsibilities in marriage. But the tendency for people to disobey, misunderstand, and distort these scriptures does not mean that these scriptures are not God's truth.

4. You may want to challenge people to think about their experiences with various authority figures and which styles of leadership they have reacted against.

5. This kind of love reflects an attitude of profound selflessness and humility, a willingness to sacrifice oneself for another.

session five

biblical responses

Objectives

A woman's responsibilities in marriage, though different from a man's, are equally important.

In this session couples will

- recognize the importance of how they respond to their spouse,
- examine what the Bible says their response should be,
- define what they see as their biblical response,
- discuss how they can support and encourage each other.

Notes and Tips

1. This session raises a topic that can be controversial—the issue of a wife's submission in marriage. It's difficult for many people to set aside preconceived ideas on this subject, and you probably will have a spirited discussion. It's important to keep the topic centered on the Scriptures. As with other difficult subjects in the Bible, we need to look at how to understand and apply what the Scripture says, even when we may not like it. And remember that this concept cannot be understood apart from the context of the subjects we studied in the first four sessions.

2. Be prepared for the discussion to go long on some questions. Look through all the questions beforehand, and mark the ones you want to be sure to discuss.

3. As the leader of a small group, you can bless your group by praying specifically for each member. Why not take some time to do this as you prepare for this session?

Blueprints Commentary

2. It is interesting to note that God applies the title "helper" to himself. "Helper" is a more lofty title in Scripture than what it typically is in our society.

4. If the group's discussion does not bring this up, you may want to share the interpretation that this phrase speaks of the need for a wife to make her home a priority.

5. These verses should not be read as contradicting each other; rather, they reveal great flexibility in how a woman fulfills her responsibilities as a wife and mother. The Proverbs 31 woman focuses on honoring her husband and caring for her family, yet she also buys a field, plants a vineyard, trades goods, and helps the poor.

8. Because we live in a world that equates submission with inferiority, a wife needs praise and honor to build her up and encourage her. Note: This principle may provide a revolutionary insight for some men and women in your group.

While we often hear exhortations for wives to submit, we rarely hear about the masculine counterpart of honor and praise.

9. Beyond the obvious negative effects on the wife, such as low self-esteem, the marriage will not be healthy and could be in danger. Also, the husband hurts himself by missing out on the blessings that come from being a God-honoring husband.

session six

making teamwork work

Objectives

Through the power of the Holy Spirit, spouses can apply the principles of teamwork in their marriage.

In this session couples will

- apply biblical responsibilities and responses to real-life scenarios,
- recognize their need for God's help in building teamwork in their marriages,
- reflect on and evaluate their experience with this course.

Notes and Tips

1. Some of the questions in this session revolve around the Holy Spirit. If you sense that this is an unfamiliar subject for anyone in your group, you may want to spend some time explaining who the Holy Spirit is and how the Spirit works in a Christian's life. A good way of explaining the Holy Spirit is to share experiences from your own life.

   On a related note, if you believe someone in your group has questions about what a Christian is, this might be a good

time to take a few minutes to explain how you became a
Christian and the difference that Christ has made in your life.
You can also refer group members to the article "Our Prob-
lems, God's Answers" (page 67) for more information.

2. People are likely to return to previous patterns of living
unless they commit to a plan for continuing the progress
made during this study. In this final session of the course,
encourage couples to take specific steps to keep their marriages growing. For example, you may want to challenge
couples to continue having a date night, as they have during
this study. Also, you may want the group to consider doing
another study from this series.

3. As part of this final session, you may want to devote some
time to planning one more meeting—a party to celebrate the
completion of this study.

Blueprints Commentary

6. The Holy Spirit is our guide and helps us understand Scripture and discern the will of God. Also, notice the prepositions
used in John 14:16 and 17. The Holy Spirit will "be *with* you
forever" and "will be *in* you." These words indicate that our
relationship with the Holy Spirit is meant to be an intimate
one.

7. Because our sinful nature is hostile to God's law, our sinful
nature will influence us to disobey the Bible.

9. Living by the Spirit means a continual dependence on the Holy Spirit for wisdom, guidance, and power. As an act of our will, we need to choose to yield to the influence of God's Spirit.

more tools for leaders

Looking for more ways to help people build their marriages and families?

Thank you for your efforts to help people develop their marriages and families using biblical principles. We recognize the influence that one person—or couple—can have on another, and we'd like to help you multiply your ministry.

FamilyLife is pleased to offer a wide range of resources in various formats. Visit us online at FamilyLife.com, where you will find information about our:

- getaways and events, featuring Weekend to Remember, offered in cities throughout the United States;
- multimedia resources for small groups, churches, and community networking;
- interactive products for parents, couples, small-group leaders, and one-to-one mentors; and
- assortment of blogs, forums, and other online connections.

who is familylife?

FamilyLife is a nonprofit, Christian organization focused on the mission of helping every home become a godly home. Believing that family is the foundation of society, FamilyLife works in more than a hundred countries around the world to build healthier marriages and families through marriage getaways and events, small-group curriculum, *FamilyLife Today* radio broadcasts, Hope for Orphans® orphan care ministry, the Internet, and a wide range of marriage and family resources.

 Dennis and Barbara Rainey are cofounders of FamilyLife. Authors of over twenty-five books and hundreds of articles, they are also popular conference speakers and radio hosts. With six grown children and eighteen grandchildren, the Raineys love to encourage couples in building godly marriages and families.